INVISIBLE WOUNDS: GUILT

The Freedom Series

James Maloney

WestBow

PRESS

A DIVISION OF THOMAS NELSON

WestBow Press books may be ordered through booksellers or by contacting:

WestBow Press
A Division of Thomas Nelson
1663 Liberty Drive
Bloomington, IN 47403
www.westbowpress.com
1-(866) 928-1240

All scripture taken from the New King James Version, unless otherwise noted. Copyright
1979, 1980, 1982 by Thomas Nelson, Inc. Used by permission. All rights reserved.

ISBN: 978-1-4908-0237-4 (sc)
ISBN: 978-1-4908-0236-7 (e)

Library of Congress Control Number: 2013912981

Printed in the United States of America.

WestBow Press rev. date: 7/22/2013

Contents

In Christ

Guilt is one of the most devastating agents the enemy of your soul will bring to bear against you. It's my belief that there are very few forces more destructive than guilt, and it is one of the main woundings of the spirit that I see many, many well-meaning people suffer under. The purpose of this booklet is to provide a brief teaching on inner-healing and how to overcome this wound of guilt.

In the short space we have here, obviously this booklet is not intended to be the sum-total on the concept of guilt and its effects. And yet, it is such a prevalent disease, I felt it was important to provide a small study on guilt and its influences, and most importantly, how to overcome it through the power of the Holy Spirit.

Whether you'd like to admit it or not, Satan has declared war on your soul—it's a prize of battle he would most definitely like to claim, and his attempt to do so is rooted in his ability to bruise and to cripple you spiritually, emotionally, mentally and physically. With guilt, the accuser attempts to malign your concept of access and acceptance before God as a born-again

Christian. Someone who is not yet born-again may be influenced by the enemy, through guilt, into believing the same lies: that God cannot accept them as they are, no matter what they've done; that God will not forgive them for the sins they've committed in the past; they are *too* guilty to accept the free gift of salvation and restoration that God is offering them.

These are all untruths. God the Father accepts us with the same level of fervency that He accepted His own Son, the Lord Jesus Christ. When we become born-again and are "in Christ," the Father looks upon us as His very own sons and daughters, just as He looks upon Christ as the Firstborn. In Jesus Christ, we have total and complete acceptance from God, no matter what. This is a fact that the enemy tries to malign.

Here are some scriptures on what it means to be "in Christ," (that is, born-again through faith in His saving power.) I have bolded the words "in Christ" for emphasis.

Romans 3:24 says we are, "justified freely by His grace through the redemption that is **in Christ** Jesus..."

"There is therefore now no condemnation to those who are **in Christ** Jesus, who do not walk according to the flesh, but according to the Spirit." (Romans 8:1) For those who are born-again, walking according to God's Spirit—and not according to their own desires (i.e., "living how they want" instead of how the Bible teaches a person should live)—there is no condemnation whatsoever from God. We have no guilt before Him.

This is the promise of God: to be free from the consequences and punishments of indwelling sin (in other words, a *lifestyle* of habitual rebellion against God's ways) as long as we submit ourselves to Jesus (that is, be "in Christ") and walk according to His ways through the help of His Spirit. If we do this, we have no guilt before Him.

Just the very next verse (Romans 8:2) says, "For the law of the Spirit of life **in Christ** Jesus has made me free from the law of sin and death." This means we have firm assurance through faith in Christ that there is no, "...height nor depth, nor any other created thing, [that] shall be able to separate us from the love of God which is **in Christ** Jesus our Lord." (Romans 8:39)

What this is all saying is, the first step in becoming guilt-free is to accept Jesus and become "in Christ." This is such a simple concept, and most of you reading this have probably already made this decision to be "in Christ"—but I take a few moments to drive the point home for those who may *not* have yet made this declaration of faith: being guiltless before God through His Son.

For those who are "in Christ" the Lord makes a covenant (a binding agreement, a pledge and a bond based on God's trustworthiness as God.) This is what He says:

> "'This is the covenant that I will make with them after those days, says the Lord: I will put My laws into their hearts, and in their minds I will write them,' then He adds, 'Their sins and their lawless deeds I will remember

no more.' Now where there is remission of these, there is no longer an offering for sin. Therefore, brethren, having boldness to enter the Holiest by the blood of Jesus, by a new and living way which He consecrated for us, through the veil, that is, His flesh, and having a High Priest over the house of God, let us draw near with a true heart in full assurance of faith, having our hearts sprinkled from an evil conscience and our bodies washed with pure water. Let us hold fast the confession of our hope without wavering, for He who promised is faithful." (Hebrews 10:16-23)

Let's take a moment and analyze these several verses. All this passage is saying is for those who are "in Christ" there is a treaty (covenant) that is made between God and man: He will make them aware of their duties before God (His laws in their hearts and minds: "This is how you should act...") And then He completely forgets that you've ever broken those laws before—as if you never rebelled against Him in the first place.

Since Jesus Christ paid the penalty for our sins, when we are "in Him"—consecrated (that means justified, sanctified, set apart: "made right") by His blood shed for our sins—we have a *right* in all boldness to come into the very sanctum of the Father (His throne room—the "Holiest" place.) Jesus is our High Priest in the house of God; He is the means by which our minds and bodies are made clean (no guilt.) He has *promised* to do this; He is faithful to do it. This makes us sons and daughters of God, free from guilt.

"Now, therefore, you are no longer strangers and foreigners, but fellow citizens with the saints and members of the household of God, having been built on the foundation of the apostles and prophets, Jesus Christ Himself being the chief cornerstone, in whom the whole building, being fitted together, grows into a holy temple in the Lord, in whom you also are being built together for a dwelling place of God in the Spirit." (Ephesians 2:19-22)

"Behold what manner of love the Father has bestowed on us, that we should be called children of God!" (I John 3:1)

Guilt is an attempt to bring shame upon you by Satan. It is a *bruising* of one's soul, wherein a conflict is created: your spirit, as one "in Christ," is the dwelling place (the "holy temple") of God's Spirit. This spirit, which resides in each one of us, is made alive and "born again" when we accept Christ as our Savior and Lord. We become a "new creation"—a different species from what we were before we accepted Christ's gift.

However, there is a separation from our spirit and our soul. Our souls are made up of our mind, will and emotions. Within this realm is where the enemy tries to bring the condemnation of guilt, in order to keep us suppressed, beat down, nominal. His attempt is to keep us under a portion of the "old ways" we used to things. The battle, then, is in your soulish life. And one of the greatest tactics of the enemy is a bruising of guilt. I believe there is no force more destructive; it is the main wounding Satan attempts to bring to us.

James Maloney

(Also, while our spirits are made new in Christ, we can still struggle within our flesh bodies; this is another tactic of the enemy: sickness, disease, infirmity. These attacks and how to overcome them are discussed in many of my other writings.)

The Serpent's Head

"When I kept silent, my bones grew old through my groaning all the day long. For day and night Your hand was heavy upon me; my vitality was turned into the drought of summer. Selah. I acknowledged my sin to You, and my iniquity I have not hidden. I said, 'I will confess my transgressions to the Lord,' and You forgave the iniquity of my sin. Selah." (Psalm 32:3-5)

The Psalmist is here lamenting about his guilt over his iniquities, but the Psalm is meant to show the absolute joy that comes from forgiveness. When we neglect or forget the beauty that is in the release of guilt over our wrongdoings, found in the forgiveness of Jesus Christ through His blood—that is, when we are found *in Him*, the joy of our salvation trumps—no, it *crushes* the controlling, limiting, hampering guilt that plagues us.

When Adam and Eve sinned, judgment was pronounced over them—they became guilty before God. What I want to highlight here is the decree that God made against the serpent who had beguiled Eve:

"… Because you have done this, you are cursed more than all cattle, and more than every beast of the field; on your belly you shall go, and you shall eat dust all the days of your life. And I will put enmity between you and the woman, and between your seed and her Seed; He shall bruise your head, and you shall bruise His heel." (Genesis 3:14-15)

The serpent is the devil, as you most likely know, and it's interesting to point out that he eats "dust"—which is poetically man's flesh, for dust is partly made of our own dead skin cells, right? So in sin, our great enemy feeds off of our flesh. His "job" is to try and consume us: guilt being just one of the many ways he tries to hamper us, biting our heels, until we trip. But how this biting often occurs is in the form of accusations and condemnation. He condemns *us* before God—"They are guilty!" He condemns God to *us*—"God doesn't mean what He says about forgiving you!" And he condemns *us* to ourselves—"You can't overcome this guilt!" This is how we are bruised by the serpent's strike.

But the connotation of "bruise" here is more unique than as it first seems. It can mean that the serpent's seed will "lie in wait" for a chance to strike out at the Man's heel, to impede His progress—and thus, impede *our* progress. The word in Hebrew means "to gape upon"—that is, "to watch out for an opening" to strike at the foot—to trip someone up. The heel is the bottommost part of the body; we're talking about our "walk" *in Christ* being bruised. For the purposes of this booklet, the enemy is "lying in wait" to find an opening to bruise us with guilt and subsequently mess up our walk *in Christ*. Sneaky. Subterfuge. Ambush. A wily snare and a trap.

When God says that the serpent will "bruise" His heel, it means a scratch. Now a scratch can be serious. It may not kill you, but it sure can thwart what you were attempting to do. For us, this can be the wound of guilt, among other weapons in the enemy's arsenal. Even though Jesus crushed Satan's head at the cross, that serpent is still able to scratch his enemy's heel (hound them, distract them, trip them up, slow down their "walk" in God.) Guilt is one such way we are scratched.

But the same word is also translated "to crush" or "to break." When God speaks of the woman's Seed (which is Christ Jesus), He will *crush* the serpent's head. That is, to take away its fangs, its potency, by destroying its head, breaking its source of power. This is not just messing up someone's walk—this means utterly smashing their means and ways, their whole authority, completely destroyed.

So the point of this little teaching is to show how we are to overcome the bruising of our heels by working *in Christ* to see the head of the enemy smashed beyond repair. We are supposed to overcome guilt (and all the works of Satan.)

Now, look, maybe you aren't consciously aware of feeling guilty about an actual act of sin—some heavy transgression against God. Perhaps you feel guilty just about the type of person you are. Say you used to be a drug addict, but the Lord got a hold of you and you quit using them. Wonderful! The actual transgression of being addicted to drugs was dealt with.

However, guilt can be a general feeling of unworthiness about the weak areas of your life to begin with. Guilt can be a generalized "put down" of your feeling of self-worth. It can be an unhealthy introspection. "I used to do abuse heroin, thank God the Lord saved me from that. But I'm still just a weakling. I must not be a very strong person to allow myself to get so messed up in drugs in the first place. How could I have been so dumb? I threw away years of my life to that stuff..."

What we're talking about here is *iniquity*—a predisposition toward a particular type of sin. Like, say, adultery is the sin; lust is the iniquity that feeds the sin. It is to "be bent" toward a sin. So in the case of our recovering addict above, he or she may have repented of the sin (using heroin) and not have dealt with the iniquity behind the sin (the bending toward addictive personality.)

So this is an open door of the enemy to bring about a wound of guilt. "So what if Jesus forgives you—you're such a terrible person to have become an addict in the first place! What's wrong with you? Other people don't become junkies. You must be inherently flawed, something isn't right with you!"

Guilt brings self-condemnation. Beating oneself up over things done in the past. This isn't healthy, this isn't the way God wants you to be. If He forgets your sins, as if they never occurred, then *you* must learn to forget them as well.

"As far as the east is from the west, so far has He removed our transgressions from us." (Psalm 103:12) The east to the west is pretty far... No matter how far you walk west across this planet—you'll never get "east." You know what I mean? It's always just west.

Now this isn't to say that our pasts shouldn't remind us of the grace and mercy of God. There are object lessons we can all learn from our mistakes in the past. "Boy, that was dumb, I won't do *that* again..."

But there is a difference between godly repentance: "Lord, I really am sorry I did that. Thanks for forgiving me, I purpose to never return to that again!" And a wounding of guilt: "I'm a miserable, sorry old wretch—God will never let this go!"

If we got down to brass tacks, guilt can really be a form of warped pride. It can turn into a pity party. Woe is me! Look how weak I am. In fact, guilt brings a need of *wanting* to be punished. "I deserve to have AIDS, I shared dirty drug needles! This is God punishing me for my sins!" That, in and of itself, can be a form of manipulation. The enemy manipulating the person through guilt; and the person trying to manipulate others (and even God) from a sense of self-reproach. And in a strange way, this is a type of false pride. When you get down to it, every sin out there, every lawless act, every lawless thought, boils down to self-pride.

The Condemning Heart

Have you ever met a person who subconsciously, or even intentionally, did things to make you reject them? Perhaps a loved one they abused or a relationship they sabotaged by passive-aggressive actions and statements. Often, these people suffer from a wound of guilt. The purpose of their actions is a form of *self-punishment*. "I'm such a broken person, I'll push you away to prove I'm such a broken person! I'll show you how messed up I am!" It's a form of self-fulfilling prophecy.

Hmmm. Take a look at Genesis 3:8: "And they heard the sound of the Lord God walking in the garden in the cool of the day, and Adam and his wife hid themselves from the presence of the Lord God among the trees of the garden."

Notice that when Adam and Eve sinned they hid from God's presence. They didn't have anything against God, so why were they hiding? They were punishing *themselves*, cutting themselves off from God.

A lot of people with a wounding of guilt say, "If I can't get anybody else to punish me, then I'll punish *myself*..." This is a definition of self-hatred.

"For if our heart condemns us, God is greater than our heart, and knows all things. Beloved, if our heart does not condemn us, we have confidence toward God." (I John 3:20-21)

If our own heart condemns us, it will affect our whole lives. Every facet of our day-to-day existence, from dealing with the people we know, our own internal thoughts, and even our relationship with God—all are tainted by a self-condemning heart. The enemy uses this to keep us wrapped up in a soulish prison of our own making, and we are hampered (in some cases, brought to naught) in the things we are supposed to accomplish in the name of loved ones, ourselves, and our God.

Now, look again, guilt *can* be useful. Proper guilt can lead us to repentance, and that's a good thing. But once we have repented, guilt should be replaced by a sense of belonging, a sense of lightness, a sense of being cleansed and set free, not bogged down in the dark shadows of the past. If guilt doesn't lead us to repentance, if we harden our hearts against it and hold out in the name of bitterness, stubbornness and rebellion or, in some cases, just downright foolishness—guilt can be turned by the enemy and used against us. Make no mistake, he'll take whatever he can get to try and thwart you in your expression to God, to others, even to your own self-worth.

Did you know a wounding of guilt can obstruct the flow of physical healing? It's a serious reason why many people out there can't get healed in their physical bodies. They labor under a false notion of their hearts condemning them—that their forgiven sins are still a hindrance to receiving the blessing of miraculous healing. Perhaps you are seeking healing and not receiving it—and perhaps one of the reasons why is a wound of guilt.

> "Then they came to Him, bringing a paralytic who was carried by four men. And when they could not come near Him because of the crowd, they uncovered the roof where He was. So when they had broken through, they let down the bed on which the paralytic was lying. When Jesus saw their faith, He said to the paralytic, 'Son, your sins are forgiven you.' And some of the scribes were sitting there and reasoning in their hearts, 'Why does this Man speak blasphemies like this? Who can forgive sins but God alone?' But immediately, when Jesus perceived in His spirit that they reasoned thus within themselves, He said to them, 'Why do you reason about these things in your hearts? Which is easier, to say to the paralytic, "Your sins are forgiven you," or to say, "Arise, take up your bed and walk"? But that you may know that the Son of Man has power on earth to forgive sins'—He said to the paralytic, 'I say to you, arise, take up your bed, and go to your house.' Immediately he arose, took up the bed, and went out in the presence of them all, so that all were amazed and glorified God, saying, 'We never saw anything like this!'" (Mark 2:3-12)

Jesus forgave the paralytic man his sins. The Lord told him: *"the penalty is remitted against you."* His debt was absolved; the man was exonerated before God. But also with that pardoning came the *sense of guilt being removed.* You know, it's entirely possible (and I believe likely) that perhaps the man never would have walked if

Jesus hadn't first told him: "You are forgiven" and removed his guilt. This is why the Lord used this miracle as an object lesson for the disbelieving scribes. The man walking *proved* the Lord forgave him and released him from his guilt.

Look, a wound of guilt hinders our operation of faith. It restricts us from receiving miracles. That's why the devil uses it against us—it bruises our heels...

Seared Conscience

The hardest kind of guilt to deal with is when you have consciously imputed guilt to someone else (blame-shifting) but subconsciously you know you're the one who's guilty. It's like you get stuck in a cycle. Throw the fault on *them*; deep down, you know you're the one to blame. So how do you cover it up? Pick someone else to blame. Rinse, repeat, recycle.

And more than that, *repeated sinning* (I mean, many times of unrepentant, habitual acts of sin) can harden the conscience wherein you don't even realize your state of "yuckiness" anymore, and yet you can still feel guilty subconsciously.

Let's look at Samson in Judges 16. He visits a prostitute in Gaza, hangs out till it's dark, and escapes from his enemies in the middle of the night. Later he falls for Delilah and shacks up with her. Yes, this is a judge of Israel...

So the Philistine leaders bribe his mistress to figure out how to zap his strength, and now Samson lies to her not once, not twice, but three times in a row, just making her look like a fool. So Delilah says, "You don't love me, you mock me with these lies." (Hmmm, ya think?) And finally, she wears him down with her persistence and he caves in, telling her the true secret behind his strength. So she gives him a haircut and his strength leaves, right? We're probably all familiar with the story here.

But notice this: when she says, "Hey, your enemies are here! Go get 'em!" Samson jumps up, all big and bad and muscular, "I'll take care of them!" and goes out to whup some Phillies. Look at Verse 20, "But he did not know that the Lord had departed from him."

How sad is that? He didn't even know *God* had left him! See, Samson continually violated his conscience through repeated sinning, and there came a day when he could no longer even tell that God's Spirit had left him. His conscience became seared by his guilt in sinning, and he could no longer even discern where God was.

Guilt can be dealt with quite easily in the mind and emotions, you know? We can blame others (not my fault, don'cha know?) or we can rationalize the guilt away (God understands, or God doesn't take it that seriously...) We can talk away our problems, or bury them under more sin.

But only the blood of Jesus Christ can cleanse the *conscience* of guilt.

> "...How much more shall the blood of Christ, who through the eternal Spirit offered Himself without spot to God, cleanse your conscience from dead works to serve the living God?" (Hebrews 9:14)

So what we're saying here is that there are basically three ways that people try to deal with guilt themselves.

One, people will try to remove their conscious/subconscious guilt by continually sinning more and more. Eventually this takes the sting out of it, and their conscience doesn't "feel" guilty anymore. This is what Paul is talking to Timothy about when he warns him of people "...speaking lies in hypocrisy, having their own conscience seared with a hot iron..." (I Timothy 4:2)

Paul is talking about people here who started off godly, but through repeated sinning, walking away from sound Christian doctrine, listening to deception from demons, they get to the point that their consciences can't even distinguish between what God considers a sin or not. Here they are, lying hypocrites (yeah, *that's* real good...) and yet they're going on about the kind of *food* a person eats, or whether or not they have to abstain from marriage: stuff you and I are like, "Well, that's pretty *duh*..."

And hey, let's be honest, that's rather gruesome imagery if you think about it. I mean, getting to the point of callousness toward guilt that your conscience gets *cauterized* by a hot poker. Wow. What a visual... How painful can that be? That's as bad as Samson getting his eyes poked out! Sure not a pleasant experience!

And yet, millions and millions of people all over the world are *doing this to themselves* on a daily basis.

The second way many people deal with a guilty feeling is just as common as the first: they blame others instead. How common is this? Well, it starts with Adam in the Garden of Eden:

"Then the Lord God called to Adam and said to him, 'Where are you?' So he said, 'I heard Your voice in the garden, and I was afraid because I was naked; and I hid myself.' And He said, 'Who told you that you were naked? Have you eaten from the tree of which I commanded you that you should not eat?' Then the man said, 'The woman whom You gave to be with me, she gave me of the tree, and I ate.'" (Genesis 3:9-12)

Poor Adam, don't you just feel embarrassed for him? Like, ooh-wow, yeah, put it off on the wife. Go ahead... Hoo-boy. That's pretty low.

But we've all been there, done that before. Don't act like you haven't. It's easy to do, throw the blame off on someone else, toss them under the bus. Not me. Didn't know. Had no clue...

Even Eve pawns off her guilt on the snake. "No, no, it's 'cause the serpent tricked me..." (Verse 13)

The problem with the blame-game is you begin to trick yourself that it's not your responsibility. You don't have to deal with the guilt, because you just flop it off on someone else. "I'm manic depressive and I take it out on my wife, but it's not my fault—my father was a jerk and used to beat me." So the root cause is never dealt with, it's just buried under the ice and snow of "it's someone else's fault."

God requires everyone to take responsibility for their actions. And most of us agree that in our society today, there is an alarming shift away from self-responsibility and owning up to one's own actions, right? We see a dramatic increase in abortions because people refuse to take the responsibility for their actions on themselves. "This baby isn't my fault—I'll get rid of it." That's harsh, but it's only too true.

Every televised criminal trial has the defendant throwing the blame on everybody but themselves. "I killed my girlfriend because she was mean to me, and my mom was mean to me, and my schoolmates were mean to me, and my dad worked too much and was never home, and they had me on Ritalin, and the military kicked me out, and my job fired me, and society has beaten me down."

I'm not trying to make light of a sad situation here, and of course, there are true victims out there, people who've had horrible things happen to them that really were out of their control. But it does not change the fact that God requires *each person* to be accountable for their own actions. We are all guilty before Him "...for all have sinned and fall short of the glory of God." (Romans 3:23)

> "In those days they shall say no more: 'The fathers have eaten sour grapes, and the children's teeth are set on edge.' But every one shall die for his own iniquity; every man who eats the sour grapes, his teeth shall be set on edge." (Jeremiah 31:29-30)

Most of us are probably familiar with that proverb about sour grapes. It basically means the children are punished for the sins of their parents—they take the same blame and are just as guilty. And while it is true that *all* are guilty before God, and that sin in itself serves as a curse that goes down through the bloodlines, each one of us have enough blame on our own to make us guilty before God.

It is true that iniquity is passed down through the generations (Exodus 20:5; 34:6-7) for "those who hate" God—in other words, the children continue disobeying the Lord just like their parents did. But let us not forget the remainder of those scriptures which say He shows "...love to a thousand generations of those who love [Him] and keep [His] commandments." (20:6)

God actually dislikes that proverb about sour grapes, and if you read Ezekiel 18, you'll see He's very clear on the subject.

The point here, for our discussion, is it does no good to blame shift—to try and pass guilt off on another, or to say, "My life is wretched because God is punishing me for my dad being such a jerk."

Your transgressions are your own, your guilt is your own—and while you may truly be a victim in some circumstances, and the fault is not your own because the sin was committed *against* you instead of *by* you—each one of us has to love God and keep His commandments for guilt to be reversed. This is the only way to be truly free of guilt, and the "sour grapes" excuse of blaming someone else isn't going to cut it when you stand before the Lord. The enemy will try to get you to pass the buck and say this is not your guilt—but it is the redeeming power of Christ's blood that washes your guilt clean.

A third way we try to do away with guilt under our own power is the age-old tactic of trying to rationalize it away. "Everybody else is doing it, why can't I?" What's wrong with a little of this and that from time to time?

Nearly all of us have had that conversation with a parent: "If everyone else jumped off a cliff, would you?" This is the "lemmings condition."

We may try to talk away our guilt, saying it's really not that bad. God overlooks little white lies. God understands my homosexual tendencies, I was just *born this way*. God knows how hard it is to stop stealing or cheating on my spouse. We try to rationalize our guilt to others. You remember those commercials for addiction help? "Honey, I can stop drinking any time..." "One more drink, it won't hurt." And then the person gets in a car accident.

Those commercials weren't far off the mark. We can get to a point where we delude ourselves that the skeletons in our closets are just little bones and dust—not some zombie waiting to come out and choke us. We have to get to a point where we view sin as God views sin: with a holy hatred. It is the little foxes that spoil the vine! (Song of Solomon 2:15)

Again, this is not an excuse for a pity-party. Woe is me! How wretched I am in my sin! Like Shakespeare once said, "We all are men, in our own natures frail, and capable of our flesh; few are angels." This doesn't get us off the hook. Guilt is not supposed to hinder you from finding truth, it's supposed to drive you to truth. The truth that is found in the redemptive works of Jesus Christ. We're not supposed to labor under guilt any more than we are supposed to sweep it indifferently under the rug—or blame someone else for it—or just give into and say, "Shucks, I've messed up already, I might as well *really* go bad..."

It bears repeating: only the blood of Jesus can truly purge the conscience from guilt!

Subconsciously Speaking

Not all guilt manifests consciously. You may not be telling yourself, "I know I'm guilty, so I'm just going to keep sinning." Or you may not be saying, "It's all *their* fault!" for specific actions you've done. And you may not be rationalizing your actions in an attempt to downplay a conscious feeling of guilt.

But how do we know if we labor under a subconscious feeling of guilt? The trap is the same, it can hinder us as much as overt guilt, and the enemy is wily enough to mess with our subconscious minds—for the end result is the same to him.

Subconscious guilt can show up in extreme forms of anxiety, fear, anger, frustration or depression. Many people who suffer with these psychological disorders labor under a subconscious form of guilt that they may not even recognize as they go about their days. Deeply buried guilty feelings can turn up in the form of anger and hostility, lashing out against someone or even oneself, without the person realizing *why* they struggle with anger. Some little tiny thing can send them over the edge, and they're suddenly "seeing red."

Now I'm not talking about the rare, occasional outburst. We can all blow it sometimes, and our emotions get the better of us. We all have boiling points, pressure points, triggers where frustrating circumstances bring out the bad in us. And that doesn't excuse the outbursts, for we are all supposed to allow the Spirit to "polish" us where we have mastery over our emotions and our bodies.

But what we're talking about here specifically is an uncontrollable, debilitating outburst—and usually the reason *why* we're angry doesn't match the level of angry that we exhibit. We go over the top. So the dog had an accident—okay, it's a dog... 'bout an IQ less than twelve and a bladder the size of a thimble. And you may not even understand *why* you kicked it, instead of just grabbing a roll of paper towels and the doggie spray. These kinds of scenarios can—though not *always*—belie a subconscious feeling of guilt. In other words, guilt may be what's feeding the irrational outburst.

Anger and hostility that's turned against the self can yield to depression, a subconscious, self-inflicted punishment. Now, again, sometimes people's depression stems from a hormonal imbalance, or the inability to deal with horrible things committed against them by someone else. Guilt is not the catch-all reason for depression. Sometimes people need deliverance from a spirit of infirmity; sometimes people need a creative miracle in their brains to bring the endocrine system online. Not *everyone* who struggles with depression also suffers under subconscious guilt.

But I'd be willing to wager it's a significant factor in many, many cases that is often overlooked.

The same goes for fear and anxiety. Sometimes the cause of an irrational fear—and I'm talking the plaguing kind of phobias that keep people locked indoors or won't let them go swimming—can stem from a root of guilt. Excessive anxiety such that a person struggles interacting with society can be a form of subconscious guilt, wherein the person is punishing themselves for an unconsciously realized action or fault or lack. Often depression goes hand in hand with eruptions of anger or deep-rooted fear, and oftentimes, it's because people are punishing *themselves*.

But here's the answer: we need to be made aware, to really know that we know that we know, that Christ has *already* received the punishment for us! Let's be strong in love here. You know what this really is? Self-punishment? It's treading underfoot the blood of Christ.

What is it that we could've done, or someone done to us, that can't be overcome by the shed blood of Jesus Christ, who was very God and very Man in one body?

> "Yet it pleased the Lord to bruise Him; He has put Him to grief. When You make His soul an offering for sin, He shall see His seed, He shall prolong His days, and the pleasure of the Lord shall prosper in His hand." (Isaiah 53:10)

Isaiah 53 is arguably the most famous chapter in the Bible, especially concerning the crucifixion of the Messiah Jesus Christ. It so poetically and powerfully describes what happened to the "Man of sorrows and acquainted with grief." (Verse 3) It talks about the "bruises" of Jesus—how the Lord crushed Him, as many translations render it, in order to provide a way for *all* of us to come back to Him. Those are the same words we were talking about earlier in the book: bruises and crushings. This is how the serpent's head was smashed—when Jesus willingly chose to be beaten and put to death, to provide a ransom for many. (Matthew 20:28; Mark 10:45) Of course, let us never forget—just as He was bruised, He was raised up!

But most of us, if we've been saved any length of time, can virtually quote from memory, "Surely He has born our griefs" all the way down to "And by His stripes we are healed." The Lord has laid on Him the iniquity of us all. (Verse 6)

So if He received the punishment, why are you punishing yourself?

Peter's Reawakening

The conscience needs to be reawakened. What I mean by that is, there are areas in all our lives that are "darkened" and need to be enlightened. (Ephesians 1:18) Most of us at some point in our lives have experienced some kind of trauma, emotional or physical. I know, some of you are probably thinking, "not just *some* kind of trauma—*all* kinds of trauma. I'm a wreck!" There's a lot of beat-up people in the world—I was one of them, once upon a time.

And see, that's another tactic of the devil. There may be reoccurrences of some similar situation that can re-stimulate the subconscious—the enemy will remind you of previous situations that brought guilt in an effort to "open up the wound" again. To rehash all the junk that went on before you came to Christ. You may even think that history is trying to repeat itself.

Sometimes these "flashbacks" are so strong it's as if the person is suffering the *identical* situation that caused the guilt all over again. In the worst cases of mental disturbances, some people are literally trapped in their minds, doomed to repeat the same scene over and over. These people can only be helped by a reawakening of their mind through an encounter with Jesus Christ.

Okay, so we know the problem. (And I'm sure most of you aren't as bad off as the people above.) But what do I mean about reawakening the conscience? There is something that needs to be revived within us that only Jesus can do. Areas of purpose and calling and destiny that the Lord "reminds" us of—His promises (and indeed, His *commandments*, to follow Him and fulfill His plan for our lives.)

We have a purpose! We have something to do that only we can do individually in the Lord. The unique callings and objectives that God has instilled in each person. We can't allow those "darkened" areas of our minds to attempt to thwart the destiny each one of us has in Christ. This is why we must overcome the wound of guilt!

Let me give you a good illustration to show what I mean. Let's talk about Peter for a few minutes.

"But Simon answered and said to Him, 'Master, we have toiled all night and caught nothing; nevertheless at Your word I will let down the net.' And when they had done this, they caught a great number of fish, and their net was breaking. So they signaled to their partners in the other boat to come and help them. And they came and filled both the boats, so that they began to sink. When Simon Peter saw it, he fell down at Jesus' knees, saying, 'Depart from me, for I am a sinful man, O Lord!'" (Luke 5:5-8)

Here's Simon's call to the ministry, for right after Jesus tells him and the others, "Follow Me, and I will make you fishers of men." (Matthew 4:19) So the Lord had a purpose for Peter: souls, so many souls that the nets would be breaking, the boat would be sinking, and he'd need to call his friends to help bring in the haul. That's a lot of souls! And we all know how Peter turned out in the end: indeed, a fisher of men!

But Peter recognizes his own guilt: "Depart from me, for I am a sinful man, O Lord!"

You can't use me, God, I'm a wretch! I've really goofed things up. I bet there's probably one or two of you out there who's said the same thing, huh?

And let's face it, Peter blows it pretty big, right? Talk about feelings of guilt!

> "Then Jesus said to them, 'All of you will be made to stumble because of Me this night, for it is written: "I will strike the Shepherd, and the sheep of the flock will be scattered." But after I have been raised, I will go before you to Galilee.' Peter answered and said to Him, 'Even if all are made to stumble because of You, I will never be made to stumble.' Jesus said to him, 'Assuredly, I say to you that this night, before the rooster crows, you will deny Me three times.' Peter said to Him, 'Even if I have to die with You, I will not deny You!' And so said all the disciples." (Matthew 26:31-35)

Bold words from Peter: I'll die before I disown you. And I'm sure at that moment, Peter was being sincere—he really intended to stick by Jesus. I doubt it was a false sense of bravado, because when Jesus was arrested, Peter did slice Malchus' ear off. (John 18:10)

Nevertheless, good intentions aside, Peter does indeed deny Christ.

> "Then he began to curse and swear, 'I do not know this Man of whom you speak!' A second time the rooster crowed. Then Peter called to mind the word that Jesus had said to him, 'Before the rooster crows twice, you will deny Me three times.' And when he thought about it, he wept." (Mark 14:71-72)

Talk about guilt! Can you imagine how Peter must have felt? Following the Lord Himself, seeing the miracles performed, listening to His teaching, seeing prophecy come to pass before his very eyes. And he upbraids Jesus for insinuating he would ever deny Christ and the power he'd seen through the Lord's hands.

Then it happens, just as Jesus said. What a whammy! Yeah, I'll bet he wept when he thought about it. *How can I do anything for God? How can I be a fisher of men, when I don't even have the courage to be associated with Him?*

A wound of guilt. Not so dissimilar from one you may be facing. Have you denied Christ? Have you failed Him once or twice or a hundred times? I know I have, and I'll bet you have too. I'm not saying there aren't *reasons* for why we feel guilty. Most of us have an awful lot of stuff to "think about and weep over."

But here's the good news! Jesus was crucified, and raised again! His blood covers Peter's faults, and yours, and mine, and *theirs*. Whoever *they* may be.

So here's miserable Peter. The Lord's been crucified; he himself is a failure, and every time he hears a rooster crow, it just reminds him how he messed up big-time. He says, "Forget this, I'm going night fishing." Like he's given up fulfilling what the Lord said he would do: be a fisher of men, so he reverts back to his old employment. (John 21)

He and three others go fishing, and all night, they don't catch a single thing. Jesus, now raised from the dead, glorified by the Father, the God-Man who saves the entire world, shows up on the shore in the morning and asks them, "What's for breakfast? Got anything to eat?"

"No."

"And He said to them, 'Cast the net on the right side of the boat, and you will find some.' So they cast, and now they were not able to draw it in because of the multitude of fish." (Verse 6)

Jesus repeats the same thing as when they first met. "Cast your net on the other side." Why? To rekindle Peter's drive to fulfill what he was called to do. Jesus had to reawaken his conscience to his call to be a fisher of men. *Remember what I told you the first time we met?*

Suddenly, Peter remembers! This happened once before! "It is the Lord!" he shouts. (Verse 7) And he won't even wait for the boat to go the three hundred feet to land. He dives into the lake fully clothed to beat the others to the shore. And yet there's a nagging sense of guilt in his mind, isn't there? He remembers, but he still needs a special touch from the Lord. *Does He really forgive me?*

They eat a nice breakfast, and Jesus knows what's bothering Peter. There's something special here that the Lord has to do for him. It takes more than just remembrance, it takes a release of guilt and shame. The conscience can't be smoothed over, locked down, or swept aside. It must be cleansed.

And Jesus has a strong conversation with Peter. The disciple denied him thrice, so the Lord asks him a question three times: "Do you love me, Peter?" Jesus is asking him, "Do you love Me, really love Me to the point of death?" Can you overcome the rooster crowing? Peter second-guesses himself the third time, and it's as if he says, "Oh, Lord, You know everything..." (Verse 17)

Now notice, Jesus reassures him he will indeed be a fisher of men. He doesn't promise him a life of cake and roses, for indeed, He tells Peter, "You know how I know you love me? You know how I know you're a fisher of men? 'Cause when you're older, you're gonna die for Me in a glorious way. You really will follow Me."

The Lord comforted Peter, restoring him unto Himself, and yet, it wasn't just tiptoeing through the tulips. But we all know what Peter accomplished in the name of his Lord, and he acquitted himself before God like virtually no other person in history, so much so that we still read of his exploits two thousand years later. Indeed the foundation of Church was laid on this fisher of men's shoulders.

His conscience was reawakened, his guilt was removed, and look what achievements Peter wrought in the name of his Savior. Praise God!

Joseph's Prisoners

Probably most of us know the story of Joseph and his brothers. In Genesis 37, we see that Israel (Jacob) loves Joseph as a favorite son, because he had him in his old age. And Israel gives Joseph a special piece of clothing to signify the boy's special place in the father's heart. (Verse 3) This tunic of many colors may have been a coat with long sleeves down to the palms and falling down to the ankles, or a richly embroidered cloak, patchworked of different colors, or perhaps different shades of one color; it might have been a robe made of silk or fine wool. The point is, this was a special, royal garment used to identify Joseph's favored position with his father—this wasn't just an old rag to go work in the fields with. It *meant* something: an identification of positional favor.

Naturally, this made Joseph's many brothers jealous. And it didn't help that Joey's all running off at the mouth about his dreams that show his brothers (and even his parents) paying obeisance to the young man. Why, even Israel's like, "Seriously? What, your mother and I are supposed to bow down to you as well? Gimme a break!"

Israel sends Joseph off on an errand, "Check on your brothers." And while he's a ways off, the brothers conspire to kill the poor kid. Reuben at least has some sort of a conscience, and he says, "Don't off him, just toss him in a pit," thinking he'd come back and rescue Joseph later.

So they take his special coat off and chuck him in a dry well, and then they *sit down to eat a meal*. Wow—talk about seared consciences!

They see some Ishmaelite traders and Judah—while not having as much of a streak of "goodness" as ol' Reuben—says, "Does us no good to kill him, let's sell him to the caravan!" And they do, for twenty pieces of silver.

Flash forward a couple decades, Joseph's risen to the right-hand man of Pharaoh, there's famine, and Jacob sends his sons to Egypt to get some grain. Joseph recognizes his brothers and accuses them of being spies, chucking them in prison.

His brethren had lost conviction (or perhaps never even had it!) over what they'd done selling Joseph into slavery; their consciences were totally seared.

So only *now* do the brothers remember their guilt, how they treated Li'l Joe some twenty odd years earlier, when he throws them in jail. It was when Joseph made them prisoners that their consciences were reawakened. Their guilt was brought to the forefront after so many years of stamping it down (by ignoring it, justifying it, or by sinning even more—look at Judah in Genesis

38!) They'd managed to blame-shift for years, but suddenly when they're kept as prisoners, it reminds them of how they'd sold Joseph into slavery.

> "Then they said to one another, 'We are truly guilty concerning our brother, for we saw the anguish of his soul when he pleaded with us, and we would not hear; therefore this distress has come upon us.'" (Genesis 42:21)

But even in the midst of this, we see how it works out in the end! It really is an amazing story, one of the coolest in the whole Old Testament. When Joseph finally reveals himself to his brothers, he says:

> "I am Joseph your brother, whom you sold into Egypt. But now, do not therefore be grieved or angry with yourselves because you sold me here; for God sent me before you to preserve life. For these two years the famine has been in the land, and there are still five years in which there will be neither plowing nor harvesting. And God sent me before you to preserve a posterity for you in the earth, and to save your lives by a great deliverance. So now it was not you who sent me here, but God; and He has made me a father to Pharaoh, and lord of all his house, and a ruler throughout all the land of Egypt." (Genesis 45:4-8)

In the end, no matter what you have done, how guilty you are, the Lord has a plan and a purpose that needs to be fulfilled through you! No one else can do it but you, for you are the only *you* in the world. (That's deep, huh?)

The reason we need to overcome guilt, to have our consciences reawakened, is so that we may be a father and a ruler through "all the land of Egypt"—our Egypt. The enemy wants to cast us in a pit, to steal *our* coat of many colors, our identity as favored children of Christ, and to sell us down the river as slaves to the baser natures. In short, to keep us guilty. We must overcome this attack, be healed of this wound by having it washed in the blood of the Lamb.

Let's close with one more short illustration. Let's talk about David.

David's Stolen Lamb

Nathan was a prophet in the king's court. And apparently one that David liked, because it's entirely possible David's son Nathan was named after this guy. But Nathan's got a bone to pick with the king, right?

For some odd reason, to start with, David felt no conviction for committing adultery and having her husband Uriah set up to be murdered.

So Nathan the prophet comes to the king with a parable:

"There were two men in one city, one rich and the other poor. The rich man had exceedingly many flocks and herds. But the poor man had nothing, except one little ewe lamb which he had bought and nourished; and it grew up together with him and with his children. It ate of his own food and drank from his own cup and lay in his bosom; and it was like a daughter to him. And a traveler came to the rich man, who refused to take from his own flock and from his own herd to prepare one for the wayfaring man who had come to him; but he took the poor man's lamb and prepared it for the man who had come to him." (2 Samuel 12:1-4)

It's interesting to note that David's conscience isn't so far seared that he just blows this off: "What a wonderful story you've told me, Nathan! Let's eat!"

No, David's all fired up. "As the Lord lives, this dude's toast!" Or something like that. (Verses 5-6) And Nathan tells him, "You are the man!" (Verse 7)

Oh, snap, talk about being put in your place... Nathan goes on: So God says, I gave you everything. Saul, your master's house and his wives, I gave you Israel, Judah, and I would've given you much more! Is this too little? You have to go and despise Me, putting Uriah to the sword, stealing his wife? Because you did this in secret, I'll give your wives to your enemy in front of the whole land! (Verses 7-12)

Talk about stern judgment. But here it is: this reawakened David's conscience. For after he hears this, he says, "I have sinned against the Lord." (Verse 13)

D'ya think? But because David acknowledged his guilt, Nathan says the Lord has put away his sins. Notice, David's not entirely off the hook here. There can be consequences for our actions, even as the Lord forgives and redeems. The sins themselves have costs, and David does pay a terrible price for the child dies.

(Thankfully we live in an era of greater grace than even David. With the blood of Jesus cleansing us, as we yield to the Spirit and purpose in our heart not to "despise" the Lord—as we recognize our guilt and He cleanses it—even our greatest losses can be turned around, and what was lost will be restored.)

And yet, as sad as this story was for David as an individual, his lesson is learned. And from this whole experience we see David wrote the fifty-first Psalm, one of the greatest prayers of repentance in the history of the earth.

"Have mercy upon me, O God, according to Your lovingkindness; according to the multitude of Your tender mercies, blot out my transgressions. Wash me thoroughly from my iniquity, and cleanse me from my sin. For I acknowledge my transgressions, and my sin is always before me. Against You, You only, have I sinned, and done this evil in Your sight—that You may be found just when You speak, and blameless when You judge. Behold, I was brought forth in iniquity, and in sin my mother conceived me. Behold, You desire truth in the inward parts, and in the hidden part You will make me to know wisdom. Purge me with hyssop, and I shall be clean; wash me, and I shall be whiter than snow. Make me hear joy and gladness, that the bones You have broken may rejoice. Hide Your face from my sins, and blot out all my iniquities. Create in me a clean heart, O God, and renew a steadfast spirit within me. Do not cast me away from Your presence, and do not take Your Holy Spirit from me. Restore to me the joy of Your salvation, and uphold me by Your generous Spirit. Then I will teach transgressors Your ways, and sinners shall be converted to You. Deliver me from the guilt of bloodshed, O God, the God of my salvation, and my tongue shall sing aloud of Your righteousness. O Lord, open my lips, and my mouth shall show forth Your praise. For You do not desire sacrifice, or else I would give it; You do not delight in burnt offering. The sacrifices of God are a broken spirit, a broken and a contrite heart—these, O God, You will not despise. Do good in Your good pleasure to Zion; build the walls of Jerusalem. Then You shall be pleased with the sacrifices of righteousness, with burnt offering and whole burnt offering; then they shall offer bulls on Your altar." (Psalm 51)

So be it! Let's be like David and acknowledge our shortcomings so that they may be cleansed, dealt with and forgotten. Don't allow an invisible wound of guilt to provide an open door to the enemy to bruise your walk with the Lord.

Let's cast off habitual sins, shake off passing blame on to others, or trying to talk away our guilt as something that doesn't hamper our daily lives of glory in the Lord.

Let the Holy Spirit move in your life and close the door to guilt. Your conscience is being awakened!

Prayer for Salvation

"Heavenly Father, I come before you today acknowledging my guilt. Against You I have sinned by leading a life and making decisions that are contrary to Your revealed will according to Your Word, the Bible, which I profess is true and real.

"I believe according to Your Word that You sent Your Son Jesus Christ, who is very God Himself, as a Man to die for my sins upon the cross. I believe that You placed the punishment for my sins upon Jesus, and my guilt upon Him, and that if I confess with my mouth and believe in my heart that Jesus is Lord of my life, and that You raised Him from the dead, I will be saved, and my guilt will be forgiven and forgotten. I acknowledge there is nothing in myself, no works that I can do, to lessen my guilt—I can only accept Your free gift of salvation and forgiveness by faith.

"Lord, I ask that You come live in my heart and change me, and rule my life according to Your will. I turn away from actions and thoughts that bring guilt upon me. I endeavor, by the power and strength of Your Spirit living inside me, to live a holy and guilt-free life, doing only that which is pleasing in Your sight.

"I accept Your gift of forgiveness and salvation, and I thank You for it. I believe I am saved by Your grace, and I will serve You alone the rest of my days."

Prayer for Releasing Guilt

"Jesus, I believe and confess that I am Yours, that I am saved by faith in You through grace, and that You have cleansed me of my sins with Your precious blood.

"I ask, God, that You would cleanse my conscience and free me from the invisible wounds of guilt and condemnation. Reawaken my conscience; show me, Lord, how You view me through the blood, that I am guilt-free of my sins when I confess them to You and ask for Your forgiveness. I know You will not withhold that from me.

"Your Word says I am forgiven, and that my sins, and the guilt of them, is forgotten. Help me to release any trappings of guilt, close any doors that the enemy would try to take advantage of, within my mind, will, and emotions. I surrender them all to You!

"Search my heart, Holy Spirit. I ask You to reveal any hidden wounds of guilt, any roots of iniquity of which I need to repent and break off, anything stemming from self-punishment and self-condemnation, or a seared conscience from unconfessed sin, or from passing blame on to others, or from trying to rationalize my guilt away.

"Cleanse me, Jesus, reawaken my conscience! Free me from the wounds of guilt, and I thank You for it. Amen!"

Printed in the United States
By Bookmasters